THE QUAKE OF '89

THE QUAKE OF '89

As Seen by the News Staff of the San Francisco Chronicle

With an introduction by
HERB CAEN
and epilogue by
RANDY SHILTS

CHRONICLE BOOKS • SAN FRANCISCO

*Cover photograph by
Vince Maggiora.
Photographs opposite title
page and on page 114
by Frederic Larson.
Photograph on page 10 by
Deanne Fitzmaurice.
Photograph at top of page
24 by Scott Sommerdorf.
Photograph at bottom of
page 24 by Jeff Reinking.
Photograph on page 108
by Eric Luse.*

A portion of the proceeds
from the sale of this book
will be donated to
earthquake relief funds.

Library of Congress
Cataloging in Publication
Data available.

Designed by John Sullivan
and Dennis Gallagher,
Visual Strategies,
San Francisco

Distributed in Canada by
Raincoast Books
112 East 3rd Avenue
Vancouver, B.C. V5T 1C8

10 9 8 7 6 5 4 3

Chronicle Books
275 Fifth Street
San Francisco, CA 94103

CONTENTS

No one was in the Geary Theatre at
5:04 p.m. October 17, when the quake
knocked the theater's ceiling and
lighting grid into a pile of rubble and
twisted steel. A performance would have
begun three hours later. *Photo by
Frederic Larson*

THE NEW SURVIVORS

By Herb Caen

Outwardly, it looks almost the same, this misty city clinging to the edge of the world. The joggers are back on Chestnut Street in the Marina. To cheers and applause from passersby on slanty California Street, the cable cars went back into service with a cheery clang, proceeding at precisely the same speed — nine miles an hour — they'd achieved in 1872, when they were invented.

At lunchtime, the dice cups rattle and bang in dozens of old-time eating and drinking establishments; shaking for the check is a lusty San Francisco tradition that no amount of shaking can halt. South of Market Street, South o' the Slot, the ancient paint-starved wooden buildings lean against each other for support along the alleys named for such long-gone but no doubt admirable ladies as Clara and Clementina, Jessie and Minna.

Let's hear it for these rickety old wrecks! For years now, their skinny frames have hung out over the streets, looking as though one good push would topple them, let alone a 7.1 earthquake, but they still stand, defying gravity, the odds and the inspectors. Truly they are the spirit of old San Francisco — bent but not broken, tipsy but on their feet, stubborn as sin and almost as defiantly ugly.

Yes, we have survived the heaviest hammer blow since the dawn of April 18, 1906 — a day that has haunted our dreams — and we have reason to congratulate one another on having survived. That's what those who lived through the '06 firequake proudly called themselves — "The Survivors." They were the aristocrats of this earthy paradise, this treasure that Mark Twain once called "heaven on the half shell."

We have lost much — too much — but we have gained much, too. The ghosts and demons of 83 years ago have been exorcised. Our city did not go up in flames, but lives have been lost, buildings have come crashing down and the damage is being counted in the billions.

The chain of hellish, difficult and sometimes even amusing events that began at 5:04:30 p.m. on Tuesday, October 17, continues to keep our small world off balance, but we have handled it well. The question that has tormented generations of San Franciscans — could we face a major catastrophe with the cocky courage and élan of our forebears? — has now been answered.

At last and at great cost, we have been validated as San Franciscans.

People live here by choice, knowing the risks. "San Francisco" and "earthquake" are almost synonymous in the minds of millions around the world, which accounts for the tremendous media interest in this city's travails — and those in Oakland — almost to the exclusion of even more stricken parts of the quake area. From the Gold Rush onward, San Francisco has been a fascinating object.

Here there is danger and adventure and "the perfectly mad people" that Rudyard Kipling admired so much that he found the city had "but one drawback — 'tis hard to leave." The pioneers set the style and tone that exist to this day. Those that had it, spent it, and not always wisely, splurging fortunes on hideous huge houses, demimondaines that were at least preferable to their horsey wives, and suckers' schemes to make another fortune.

There was and is a certain wildness in the air, a "tomorrow we die" attitude based on the unspoken awareness that the earth could open up in the next instant and swallow it all — from the baroque palaces of Nob Hill to the gaming houses of the Barbary Coast. That attitude has carried over to this day. It may account for the city's hedonistic devotion to good food and strong drink (the old town's fabulous eating troughs were famous around the world long before the idea of a "celebrity chef" was born).

A headstrong, careless city dancing forever on the edge of disaster to the tune of "The Grizzly Bear," or, more appropriately, Ravel's "La Valse," with its dissonant earthquake of an ending. The knowledge that disaster lurks just below the earth's crust may account for our high incidence of alcoholism, of suicides off the elegantly aloof Golden

Gate Bridge, of wild excesses in our ways of living, laughing, lying and dying.

Under its polished overlay of cynical sophistication, San Francisco is still a frontier town. The narcissism that so annoys and mystifies "the outsiders," a term of derision, comes from self-awareness. We know we are different. We like being different. Sometimes we go to outlandish lengths to be different, simply to shock "the outsiders."

We don't think we are odd for living right here in Quiver City. We think people like Jesse Helms, Jim Bakker and Dan Quayle are odd.

These days shook our snug and sometimes smug little world and allowed the outside world, the one we like to keep at bay, to come in and look us over with its Cyclopean camera eye. We are not the same city or the same people we were the instant before H-Hour on Q-Day.

It is considered hip or at least fashionably insouciant to reiterate that it was not "The Big One," it was just the Almost Big One or the Little Big One. For those who died and those who lost everything, it was The Big One, period.

In some ways, the day after the earthquake did seem like the first day of the rest of our lives. The people held up admirably, and worked together with spirit and strength, but everyone was in shock. The city we love had taken a blow to the head that left it groggy. Still on its feet, yes, but the haymaker came frighteningly close to a knockout.

When our vision cleared, we saw San Francisco in a clearer light. It was like rediscovering our feelings for this unpredictable, wild and wildly fascinating place. We realize afresh the joys and dangers of living here, and we reaffirm our belief that it is worth the gamble, however great. We know the pluses — the history, the traditions, the laughter on the hills, the freshness of the constant winds of change. And we have been reminded, with a sharp jolt, of the minuses.

These we can do something about. "Earthquake preparedness" is no longer a phrase to glaze the eyes. Too boring, my dears. Yes, killingly so, old chums. Now let's buckle down and see if we can atone for our sins of omission. Our sins of commission we know all too well.

5:04:30 P.M., OCTOBER 17, 1989

T he mood of the crowd awaiting the first pitch that warm San Francisco afternoon at Candlestick Park was playful. It felt good to be alive. It was better than good. It was simple. ¶ And then it got complicated. ¶ It was just after 5. John Crayton, the 42-year-old captain of the Goodyear blimp floating 2,000 feet above the stadium, suddenly didn't understand what was happening. ¶ The blimp vibrated — just a jiggle, really — but that could have been the result of a passing plane. What puzzled Crayton was that the blimp suddenly lost its TV link with the park below. ¶ Crayton cursed to himself. He thought someone had tripped over a cord and pulled a plug — "a director could lose his job for that," he thought. ¶ Five seconds. Ten seconds. Fifteen seconds. ¶ To the north, Crayton saw a green flash under Interstate 280 — transformers exploding. The blimp crew regained contact with a technician on the ground. ¶ "Earthquake," he said.

SHOCK

ABOVE AND OVERLEAF: With no electricity in Candlestick Park, 60,000 puzzled fans wait to be told what to do. On the field, players, coaches and their families mill about in the gathering darkness. *Photos by John O'Hara*

PAGE 3: Elation before Game 3 of the 1989 World Series turns to stunned silence and confusion. "My heart stopped," said a spectator who was sitting at the top of the stadium under a curved concrete lip. *Photo by Brant Ward*

LEFT: There are few signs of panic. Almost as soon as the trembling stops, the crowd lets out an ironic cheer. In the confines of Candlestick, no one realizes the magnitude of the disaster. *Photo by Brant Ward*

6

John Crayton
*Captain,
Goodyear blimp*

*"The Bay Bridge
was just —
broken. The top
deck was down
into the lower one.
I thought,
'Oh, my God.'"*

LEFT: A weak link proves the undoing of the San Francisco – Oakland Bay Bridge, a major artery across San Francisco Bay. A 50-foot section of the upper deck collapses onto the lower deck. One person is killed. *Photo by Deanne Fitzmaurice*

BELOW: Uncertainty prevails as traffic on the bridge stops abruptly. Some are able to turn around and drive back; others flee on foot. *Photo by Brant Ward*

B A Y   B R I D G E

Buck Hall
Metal worker

"The tunnel was moving, the bridge was moving, all the cars were sliding around like they were on ice. The suspension cables on the bridge were swinging back and forth, like a giant harp somebody was playing. Then everyone started slowly driving off the bridge, at about 25 miles an hour. It wasn't fast enough for me. All I wanted was to get off that bridge."

ABOVE: Cars dangle over the bay after the upper deck, right, smashed down and partially through the lower deck. *Photo by Steve Ringman*

LEFT: Dazed commuters peer at a roadway suddenly careening downhill onto the lower deck. *Photo by Steve Ringman*

Death struck at random

People died, or didn't, because of where they were when the world broke apart.

Bruce Stephan was sure he was going to die. The engineer was returning home to San Francisco with a co-worker on the upper deck of the Bay Bridge when his car began to jump up and down. Then the portion of the bridge beneath them collapsed. The car plunged from the upper deck to the damaged lower deck, and nearly into the bay.

"We were falling through the bridge, and there was nothing to catch us," he said.

Stephan turned to his co-worker and told her, "Janice, we are going to die."

Suddenly a piece of the gnarled bridge caught the car, and the pair dangled precariously above the water. "I saw water below us," said Stephan. "I felt for sure we were going into the bay."

But the car moved no farther.

Peter Gray was giving dictation at a commercial building at Sixth and Bluxome streets in San Francisco when his office wall "just blew out like an explosion," leaving "nothing but blue sky" two feet from his chair. The wall cascaded onto parked cars filled with Gray's co-workers, who were leaving for home. Jeffrey Choi, a sample cutter, was one of the five who died under the rubble.

Scott Dickinson, a 3½-month-old infant, was killed in the collapse of an apartment building in San Francisco's Marina District. Only minutes before, his father, Walter, had waved good-by to his wife and son and pedaled off for a spin around the neighborhood. When he returned, his home was destroyed, his son dead and his wife seriously injured.

RIGHT: Across the bay in Oakland, a 1½-mile section of the double-deck I-880 freeway collapses, trapping or crushing motorists on the lower deck. "You could hear it ripping," said a truck driver. "When the top zigged, the bottom zagged."

ABOVE LEFT: Shock waves turn the hard mud base of San Francisco's Marina District into mush, tossing houses off their foundations and into the streets. *Photo by Vincent Maggiora*

BELOW LEFT: An apartment building crushes a parked car in the Marina, where broken gas lines would later spark voracious fires. *Photo by Vincent Maggiora*

ABOVE RIGHT: Hundreds of Marina residents, evacuated from collapsing buildings, wait at a school shelter for word on the fate of their homes. *Photo by Brant Ward*

BELOW RIGHT: Brick facades crumble all over San Francisco. *Photo by Brant Ward*

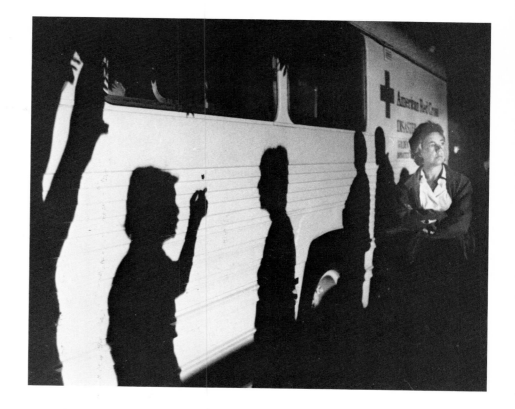

ABOVE: On fashionable Union Square, scores of windows shatter at the I. Magnin department store, raining shards of glass onto sidewalks. *Photo by Frederic Larson*

RIGHT: When the shaking stops, reassuring hugs help survivors through the first frightening moments of silence. *Photo by Frederic Larson*

LEFT: In the unstable Santa Cruz mountains to the south, cabins are shoved off foundations; many slide down hills. *Photo by Steve Castillo*

RIGHT: Support columns pierce Highway 1 near Watsonville, 77 miles south of San Francisco and 13 miles from the earthquake's epicenter. *Photo by John O'Hara*

BELOW: An older Watsonville
house is severely damaged.
Photo by John O'Hara

RIGHT: Deep cracks
open in isolated portions
of the Santa Cruz
mountains, mystifying
geologists and raising
fears of landslides. "I
can't stop shaking," said
one resident. "I guess
I'm surviving, but I'm
scared." *Photo by
Deanne Fitzmaurice*

ABOVE: Old bricks give way in
downtown Hollister, 80 miles south of
San Francisco. Weightlifters on the first
floor of the Odd Fellows Hall find
themselves suddenly in the open air.
Photo by John O'Hara

CONFUSION

Running in slow motion

Arlette Smith, a Walnut Creek social worker, was on the Bay Bridge, only a few hundred feet from the section of upper deck that broke loose. People came running back in her direction, screaming that the bridge had collapsed.

Smith assumed that meant the bridge was actually in the process of collapsing. She concluded she was going to die. In her high heels, she ran back toward Yerba Buena Island, which divides the two spans of the bridge.

In spite of her instincts howling on behalf of self-preservation, she noticed a little boy lost on the roadway. She scooped him up and ran on. "It was like a dream where you run and run and you don't seem to move at all."

She spent the night with 17 other bridge refugees in a Navy lieutenant's home, then made her way home to Contra Costa County. The boy's family retrieved him. They were safe — or what passed for safe before 5:04 p.m. on Tuesday.

OVERLEAF: "The whole town, the buildings, were swaying together like they were dancing," said one observer in Union Square. *Photo by Frederic Larson*

RIGHT: A victim of falling glass from Union Square department stores is taken to a hospital. Bloody shards litter sidewalks. *Photo by Frederic Larson*

BELOW: Throngs at downtown bus stops, awaiting now-powerless trolleys, begin the long walk home. Some people go into the streets with hand-lettered signs, asking for rides. *Left photo by Michael Maloney, right photo by Frederic Larson*

LEFT: Passersby keep an eye on shattered windows and crumbling masonry. *Photo by Frederic Larson*

TOP: Electrically driven trolleys stand abandoned where they stopped when the power went off. Diesel buses continue to run, but drivers don't collect fares. A passenger uses a cellular telephone. *Photo by Steve German*

BOTTOM: Long lines form at pay telephones when tens of thousands of commuters are stranded. *Photo by Jeff Reinking*

ABOVE AND RIGHT:
Major hotels light
candles and try to calm
disoriented tourists.
"People were sitting on
benches in the square,
drinking champagne,
having a party," said a
visitor from Florida.
When it is time to turn
in, hotel personnel with
flashlights lead guests to
their rooms.

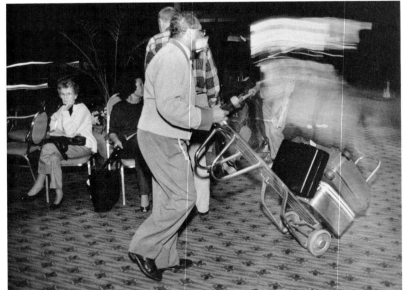

Christine Goldapp
West German tourist

"We would like to go

now. In Germany, there

are no earthquakes."

BELOW: The Pacific
Stock Exchange opens
the next day without
power; traders conduct
business by candlelight.
Photo by
Scott Sommerdorf

Heart on a roller coaster

We ate salad and bread and ice cream by candlelight and waited for the children to call. The little portable radio talked scratchily of collapsed buildings, crushed freeways, fires and threats of looting. We talked softly, if at all, as though at a funeral for the end of the world.

By 9:15, the now-white moon silvered the water and bathed the city. The last child reported in safe. I suddenly felt secure in our warm cave. We had all survived. Several windows were cracked. Flakes of paint and plaster dotted the floor from the worst earthquake of my lifetime. But we had survived!

In the bright morning, the elation grew. We were still without gas or electricity. I took a cold shower, ate a cold muffin, drank a glass of lukewarm milk and went without shaving. There was an air of camping out — a feeling of freedom and adventure.

On the way to work, we drivers scrupulously took our turns at intersections where the signals stared blankly. No longer were we hell-bent motorists encased in steel, but real human beings with feelings for each other. What surprised me was that they were as decent as I. Anarchy, I thought, works.

At Jones and Eddy streets, in the heart of San Francisco's Tenderloin District, a man in tattered jeans with a long beard was directing traffic. I gave him a thumbs-up and a grin as I passed, and he returned them in kind. Brothers we were for that moment — brothers, he and I.

I relished the exhilaration that escape from danger brings. The routine of my days had been shattered. How young and vital I felt. How more precious life becomes when others are losing theirs.

Yesterday morning, the power was still off. Another cold shower, another cold breakfast. The adventure was beginning to pall. On the way to downtown San Francisco, most of the signals were working. At Taylor and Geary, a cab driver cut me off. I cursed him silently.

From a column by ART HOPPE, The Chronicle, *October 20, 1989*

LEFT: People gather together, as they did after the 1906 quake, and share experiences. *Photo by Scott Sommerdorf*

RIGHT: Marina District residents leave messages for one another on utility poles after they are forced to evacuate their homes. *Photo by Brant Ward*

RICH BODNY
I AM AT THE MIDDLE
SCHOOL UP THE STREET—
RED CROSS CENTER —
PLEASE COME —
NOT CROSS

HORROR

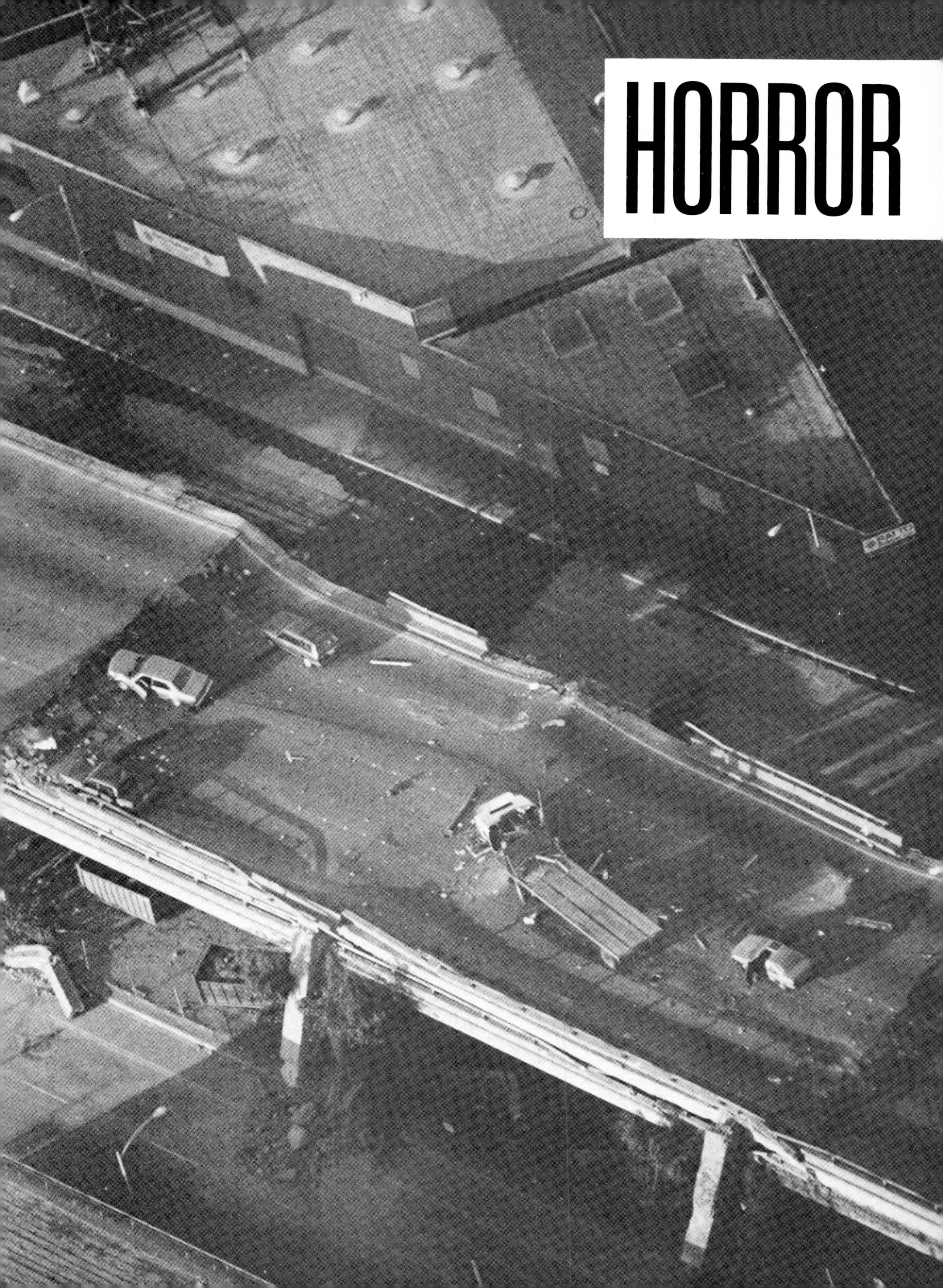

OAKLAND

Thomas Stevens
*Eyewitness to
I-880 collapse*

*"It was like a big,
giant, long ocean
wave, and behind
each wave a
portion of the
freeway collapsed.
I just started
crying. Then I
started thinking of
all those people on
the freeway and I
said, 'Please, God,
let that freeway
hold.' But I knew it
wouldn't hold."*

OVERLEAF: The top deck
of I-880 in Oakland has
thundered down onto
the lower deck in huge
sections of concrete.
*Photo by
Deanne Fitzmaurice*

BELOW: There were cars in that impossibly small space, and there were people inside the cars.
Photo by Deanne Fitzmaurice

LEFT:
"I saw smoke and cement. . . . I couldn't believe what I was seeing."
Photo by Tom Levy

ABOVE: Fearing that aftershocks or any vibration could cause further collapse of the swaying freeway, rescue workers ban helicopters from the I-880 area and restrict vehicle movement. *Photo by Tom Levy*

A tangle of life and death

A little after 5 p.m. that Tuesday, Alvin Wong, a San Francisco police officer, was thinking lazy thoughts about the World Series as he followed his customary route home from the city to the East Bay. Suddenly his Honda Accord bucked and veered. Ahead of him, a huge truck disappeared as the road beneath it dropped "like an elevator."

The place the quake hit hardest was this 1½-mile stretch of Interstate 880 in Oakland, known as the Cypress structure. Disaster became tragedy as scores died on a bit of road that could normally be traversed in 90 seconds.

Stunned by what he had just seen, Wong got out of his car and peered toward the broken edge of pavement where the truck had been swallowed up.

The stench of spilled gas, burning tires and scorched asphalt was everywhere. Black smoke seeped up from the lower deck through huge cracks in the road.

"I had just seen something so horrendous. One minute cars and trucks were there, the next second they're gone, swallowed in a cloud of dust."

ABOVE: "We heard people screaming like hell everywhere. The people on top (of the freeway) we could help, but there was nothing we could do about the people underneath," said a neighborhood man. *Photo by Steve Ringman*

LEFT: Rescuers using listening devices and infrared cameras to detect body heat think they hear the cry of a human voice in the rubble. It turns out, eerily, to be the CB radio from a vehicle in the wreckage. *Photo by Tom Levy*

Bill McElroy
*Neighborhood
rescuer*

*"People were
howling, some of
them from caves
of concrete."*

RIGHT: "All around you
could hear voices saying,
'I'm hurt, I'm hurt, help
me,'" said a witness.
The final death toll on
I-880 was 41.
Photo by Tom Levy

Ordinary people, extraordinary acts

A stunned crowd had quickly gathered on the street below the smoking freeway. "They were just standing there staring," said Bill McElroy, a neighbor who had driven to the scene at breakneck speed. "I told them, 'We better get us organized. There's people up there that need us.' "

It was an unlikely earthquake rescue committee: perhaps 50 people, blacks and Latinos, blue-collar workers from nearby businesses, parents and children, many from the projects — not a firefighter or a paramedic among them.

"Go home and get ladders and some rope!" McElroy ordered. "Bring me some wire cutters, jacks, power saws, any tools you've got!"

And that is what the people did, even though they realized that a big quake is always followed by aftershocks and an aftershock could bring the devastated freeway crashing and crushing the rest of the way down.

In a matter of seconds the neighborhood literally began reaching out to those trapped in the ruins.

John Crayton
Captain,
Goodyear blimp

"Flames were

shooting 200 to

300 feet in the air,

and it wasn't

slowing down."

LEFT: As the evening
sky darkens, people
can see the fire in the
Marina from all over
San Francisco.
Photo by Steve Ringman

37

RIGHT: A devastated building lurches into the street. Another home burns behind it. *Photo by Frederic Larson*

LEFT: In the Marina, some buildings buckle, some collapse or burn. Residents rush to prop up three- and four-story structures that have tumbled into the street. *Photo by Vincent Maggiora*

ABOVE AND LEFT: When broken mains cut off water for Marina fire hydrants, seawater is pumped from the bay. *Photos by Vincent Maggiora*

THE MARINA

Vic Giannini
Resident

"I saw a man dive into

what was the fourth floor

of a building looking for

survivors. . . . He came out

empty handed."

SANTA CRUZ MOUNTAINS

Steve Underwood
Carpenter

"Our house dropped six inches. We're hanging over

an 80-foot ravine. It's dangerous. We're camping out

in the woods with our friends."

TOP: A storage house is knocked down a hillside in the Santa Cruz mountains. *Photo by Deanne Fitzmaurice*

BOTTOM: Brick buildings in downtown Los Gatos, 50 miles south of San Francisco, are checked for structural damage. *Photo by Deanne Fitzmaurice*

ABOVE: Isolation is part of the beauty of the Santa Cruz region, but it becomes dangerous when Highway 17, the county's main artery north to the Bay Area, is closed by landslides. *Photo by Steve Castillo*

A waking nightmare

Ryan Moore was taking a nap in his bedroom in the Santa Cruz mountains. The jolt awakened him, and the house began a plunge 100 feet down the side of a cliff. Moore closed his eyes and pulled the covers around himself. In seconds he was at the bottom of the hill; his house had turned into matchsticks, but he was still in bed, only scratched and bruised.

RESCUE

ABOVE: Rescuers cut
mangled rebar with
torches, searching
feverishly for trapped
motorists on Oakland's
I-880. *Photo by
John O'Hara*

OVERLEAF: The injured
are plucked from
teetering buildings in
the Marina District.
*Photo by
Scott Sommerdorf*

LEFT: Exhausted rescue workers rest. The search for survivors amid twisted steel and concrete is emotionally as well as physically draining. *Photo by Tom Levy*

RIGHT: Forty feet above the ground, workers build a scaffolding to hold up sections of the freeway that threaten to crash down. *Photo by John O'Hara*

Ruthless lifesaving

Six-year-old Julio Berumen was trapped in his family's mangled car, which was jammed into little more than a crevice left when the top tier of the double-decked freeway I-880 dropped.

The boy was given morphine. Then, in a space better suited to spelunking than delicate surgery, a surgeon used a chain saw to cut through the body of a woman in the car to gain access to the boy, whose right leg was inextricably pinned by the weight of the wreckage. Amid the dust and gore, the surgeon amputated the boy's leg below the right knee.

Five hours of ruthless effort had saved the boy's life. Dr. James Betts, chief of pediatric surgery and director of the Pediatric Trauma Center at Children's Hospital in Oakland, had become a hero of the earthquake.

LEFT: "People were carrying the wounded on their backs down ladders, sometimes 40 feet or more. These people never knew whether the freeway was going to collapse again," said a witness.
Photo by Tom Levy

ABOVE: Rescue workers move through pockets of debris, calling out, "Is there anybody there? Is there anybody there?"
Photo by Tom Levy

O A K L A N D

Gregory Hibbard
Police officer

"I knew . . . that there were dead people

inside. I wondered who they were, what

they had looked like, where they were

going. It was numbing."

Richard Von Riddle
Volunteer rescuer

"It's like hell up there — people have lost their families up there. There's always hope of life. If I was trapped, I know others would do this for me."

RIGHT: A temporary first-aid station is set up near the pancaked freeway. *Photo by Tom Levy*

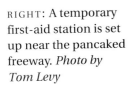

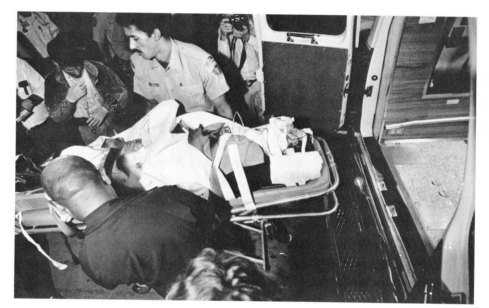

RIGHT: Near the freeway collapse, rescuers pull survivors and bodies from the rubble. *Photos by Tom Levy*

The man who refused to die

At 6 a.m., well before sunrise, Steven Whipple, an engineer for the California Department of Transportation, was suspended in a cherry picker in the light rain outside a pancaked stretch of I-880. Checking for structural instability, he let his flashlight play across the face of a corpse, newly revealed, trapped in a crushed Chevrolet Sprint. He moved the light away, brought it back again. The corpse had moved its hand away from its face.

Despite official pessimism about finding any survivors inside the crushed structure, those allowed to work at the disaster site were determined to work anyway. Those not allowed to work had prayed. And those who could neither work nor pray had hoped.

Four hours after his discovery — 89 hours after the collapse of the expressway — to windswept cheers, rescue workers extracted the last spark of life from the tottering rubble. The survivor's name was Buck Helm. When the freeway collapsed, he had been proceeding at moderate speed to a poker parlor.

The 57-year-old diabetic ship's clerk spent his ordeal, seat belt fastened, slumped in the front seat of his car, the front of which had been flattened by a falling slab of concrete. But a steel beam shielded the passenger compartment. As his rescuers brought him down, he waved to the crowd.

At the hospital, physicians were cautious. His injuries were not life-threatening: bruised lungs, three broken ribs and a skull fracture. But he was severely dehydrated, and his kidneys had shut down in his body's struggle to slow the dying process. A few days later, doctors gave him a thumbs-up. Buck Helm would survive.

He was alive because, his friends said, he was "too ornery to die."

Those who had not wept before wept the day they brought out Buck Helm.

ABOVE AND LEFT:
Buck Helm is gently lowered to the ground in a basket. His rescuers break into cheers.
Pool photos by Angela Pancrazio, Oakland Tribune

BELOW: Specially
trained dogs are walked
through buildings in the
sagging Marina District,
searching for bodies or
survivors. *Photo by
Brant Ward*

Split-second choices

At Oakland Fire Station No. 3, Lieutenant John Ironside, an 18-year veteran, was preparing to sit down to what he hoped would be an uninterrupted meal — chicken piccata, pasta, salad and three hours of World Series baseball as dessert. When the quake hit, someone yelled and everyone crowded under an archway next to the kitchen. The boiling pasta water slopped onto the floor.

Almost at once, the engine rolled — the call was a building in danger of collapse and a gas leak. But when Ironside saw the mangled I-880 freeway, he chose to ignore the original call.

"I had a number of decisions to make — the first was whether the structure was sound enough to attempt to rescue. Right or wrong, I made a decision to proceed. We threw our 100-foot aerial ladder up to climb to the top level."

In the first chaotic moments after the earthquake, either Ironside's men or another crew pulled commercial banker Michael Harp to safety.

On a day of split-second differences between living and dying, if anyone teetered on the knife's edge, it was Harp.

I-880 was rolling and cracking like a gigantic brittle bullwhip as Harp drove across it at ever-increasing speeds, trying to stay in front of the devastation. "I would dip down, go into a gully, and then I'd come out of one of those dips and I'd be airborne for a couple of seconds.

"The freeway was literally falling apart at this point. I could see that the section ahead looked like it would remain intact, and I was praying, 'Dear God, just please let me get there.' "

Just as his wheels touched what he thought would be a safe haven, the section he was on began to fall, turning into a sort of "ramp or ski-jump, and the car shot straight up and was flying through the air . . . and the next thing I could see I was heading downward toward the pavement."

Harp's car came to rest upside down, about 25 feet from where the roadway broke.

Although Harp's left arm was now useless, he unfastened his seat belt and squeezed out onto the freeway. His ribs were broken. His shoulder was fractured. Unable to stand without losing consciousness, Harp lay there until a ladder appeared, and two firefighters climbed up.

"We need to get you down from here because this structure could go," they explained, as if Harp needed to be persuaded.

OAKLAND

Jenayvonne Johnson
Resident of condemned building

"Every dime we had went

into that apartment. . . .

We're broke. We're hurt.

We're disgusted, but we

haven't lost hope."

RIGHT: In the Marina, a school becomes a Red Cross shelter for hundreds of displaced residents. *Photo by Nancy Wong, special to The Chronicle*

BELOW: A lunch of donated food is served in Watsonville. *Photo by Deanne Fitzmaurice*

S A N   F R A N C I S C O

Cindy Beckett
Flight attendant

"I got out with what I have on and an
overnight bag and can't get back into my
apartment. . . . It's the last thing you
would ever think would happen to you."

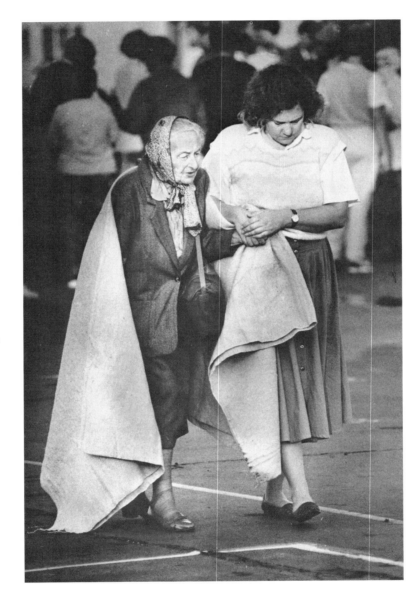

RIGHT: When the earthquake hit, people knew what to do. Ordinary citizens came to the rescue, offering help and sometimes even champagne. *Photo by Frederic Larson*

RIGHT: A volunteer comforts a woman who waits to hear about her husband's condition. Her sister had died on the Bay Bridge. *Photo by Liz Hafalia*

ANGUISH

ABOVE: Valuables are quickly moved out of tottering houses in Los Gatos, 50 miles south of San Francisco. *Photo by Michael Maloney*

OVERLEAF: Five people are killed when the brick walls of a six-story San Francisco building tumble down, crushing cars in a narrow street below. *Photo by Steve Ringman*

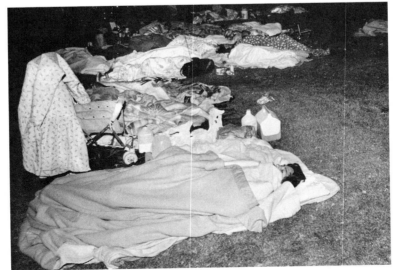

LEFT: Farther south in the farming center of Watsonville, 500 people are forced into a half-dozen tent villages; 1,000 are in shelters. *Photo by Steve Castillo*

BELOW: Watsonville
suffers extensive
damage, with 250 houses
knocked from their
foundations.
Photo by John O'Hara

SAN FRANCISCO

Carl Nolte
Chronicle reporter

"People often ask,

'How can I tell when

there is an earthquake?'

and Californians always

answer: 'You will just

know. You will know.'"

TOP LEFT: Fearing further collapse of Oakland's shattered I-880, police evacuate neighborhoods surrounding the freeway. *Photo by John O'Hara*

LEFT: Cleanup can be daunting in apartments that seem to be turned upside down. *Photo by Vincent Maggiora*

ABOVE: Some older
San Francisco
apartments sustain
heavy damage.
Photo by Brant Ward

ABOVE: Rescue workers spray-paint SEARCHED as they move through battered buildings in the Marina District; many structures are then quickly demolished to avoid further danger. *Photo by Eric Luse*

LEFT: A survivor mourns the death of two friends in the Marina. *Photo by Darcy Padilla*

RIGHT: Two people stand in front of where they once lived. The building will be torn down. *Photo by Frederic Larson*

Robert Makinson
Marina District

"I went for a walk and when I came

home the building had collapsed.

I lived there 20 years."

TOP: Sagging pavement and homes on Chestnut Street in the Marina. *Photo by Darcy Padilla*

BOTTOM: Neighbors engage in a frantic scramble to retrieve whatever they can in the 15 minutes they are allowed back in their buildings. *Photo by Vincent Maggiora*

LEFT: Some Marina apartment dwellers are allowed into their homes long enough to retrieve a few treasured belongings. *Photo by Brant Ward*

Castles built on sand

As daylight came after that first terrible night, Marina District residents saw that the quake had done great damage to their elegant neighborhood. The culprit was something called liquefaction. The Marina is built on 165 acres of landfill. Agitated by sufficient seismic turbulence, fill turns into a kind of sandy Jell-O.

As health buffs jogged past the listing buildings, a phalanx of inspectors moved more slowly through the Marina. Green permit: safe building. Yellow permit: dangerous building. Red permit: uninhabitable.

TOP: Building and fire inspectors try to assess which buildings are safe. In many cases men and women weep when told they will not be allowed beyond the yellow police lines. *Photo by Frederic Larson*

LEFT: City officials fear there are dozens of elderly Marina residents, alone and confused, living in damaged homes. In some cases, workers have to take frightened residents out of their homes by force. *Photo by Brant Ward*

RIGHT: "It was like it was blasted down," said a Marina survivor. *Photo by Eric Luse*

15 minutes to salvage a lifetime

E ileen Brady, 79, and her sister Eleanor, 80, had received a red notice that meant they would have 15 minutes to get what they needed out of Eileen's Marina District apartment of 20 years.

"Fifteen minutes isn't much time," said Eleanor, a retired teacher from Salt Lake City who was in the middle of a three-month visit with her sister when the quake struck. "But for us, I think it's a little more difficult. At our age, we're built for endurance, not speed."

Eleanor looked at the long list she and her sister had made of items they hoped to retrieve: medications, checkbooks, bank and tax records, address books, clothes. And, if time allowed, some of the Hummel figurines, ivory statues and Oriental vases and prints Eileen had collected from around the world during her 30 years in the Army.

It began to rain. "God isn't being very helpful, is he?" said Eileen, leaning on her cane. She looked up at the gray sky. "Look, God, we're trying to cooperate. Could you?"

New friends materialized to help the sisters enter their neighborhood. Strangers gathered to help. For half an hour, the sisters watched as volunteers moved whatever they could out of the crumbling apartment and into a pickup truck. The carefully prepared list became irrelevant in the chaos.

People found strength they didn't know they had to lift china cabinets and filing cabinets out of the crumbling apartment. The workers had to dodge clothes flying out of windows of nearby buildings. The rain continued to fall.

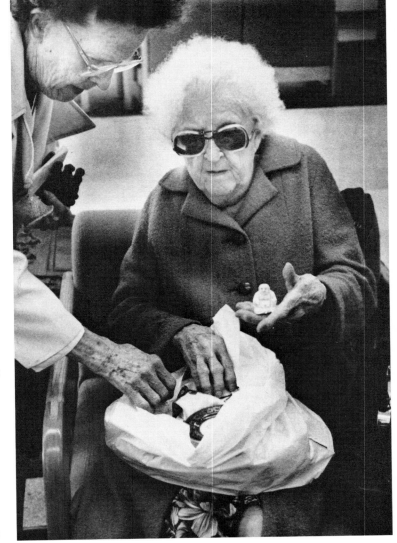

LEFT: Eleanor Brady, left, helps her sister, Eileen, examine belongings retrieved from their listing apartment.
Photo by Liz Hafalia

RIGHT: Many apartment buildings appear undamaged from the street, but residents say foundations are cracked and their apartments ravaged. *Photo by Brant Ward*

BELOW: At a Marina shelter, two friends embrace, relieved to find each other. *Photo by Frederic Larson*

ABOVE: Displaced residents stand in line for breakfast at a Red Cross shelter. *Photo by Frederic Larson*

LEFT: Joe DiMaggio, a longtime resident of the Marina, stands in line to find out the condition of his home. He learns his house is fine. *Photo by Frederic Larson*

RIGHT: Colored slips of paper tell the fate of Marina homes. *Photo by Brant Ward*

LEFT: Marina neighbors wait for information in long, slow lines. *Photo by Frederic Larson*

RIGHT: A now-homeless survivor camps near the Palace of Fine Arts. *Photo by Vincent Maggiora*

BELOW: Tenants wait wearily. *Photo by Brant Ward*

Frances Brejska, 92
Marina District

"My philosophy is, What can you do if it is fated? Anyway, this is nothing compared to what I went through with the Communists in Czechoslovakia."

BELOW: Shopping carts are hastily loaded up with possessions. *Photo by Frederic Larson*

TOP: Some buildings rated too dangerous to enter are destroyed immediately, and tenants' belongings are buried in the rubble. *Photo by Frederic Larson*

BOTTOM: Marina residents quickly retreat from endangered blocks, loaded with any belongings they can salvage. *Photo by Eric Luse*

REGROUPING

Salvaging broken lives

Cities seem as solid and permanent as any of the works of man, but an earthquake shows how brittle and provisional they are, how dependent on fragile transportation, power and communication webs that are broken with absurd ease when the earth twitches. There is nothing like a natural disaster to rob a city of its strut, its nothing-can-touch-me sense of braggadocio.

Stanley Norman, Jr.

"How can you be mad? It's nobody's fault. It's San Andreas's fault. I still love this place. . . . This is home. I wouldn't want to live anywhere else, even after the earthquake."

TOP: Clothing and blankets are distributed to newly homeless Marina residents. *Photo by Darcy Padilla*

BOTTOM: Morning coffee is served at a Red Cross shelter. *Photo by Darcy Padilla*

RIGHT: A middle school classroom becomes a dormitory. *Photo by Frederic Larson*

Barbara García
*Community clinic
executive director*

*"We're talking
about people with
no resources, no
money for food
and no money for
health care."*

ABOVE: Watsonville
residents line up
for water. *Photo by
Chris Stewart*

LEFT: Families forced to
live in tents search
through piles of donated
clothing in Watsonville.
*Photo by
Deanne Fitzmaurice*

RIGHT: Kirt Manwaring
and Matt Williams of the
San Francisco Giants
visit an evacuation
shelter in San Francisco.
Photo by Brant Ward

Leo Bazile
Oakland city councilman

*"Before the World Series, we
expected the media to talk
about our fine restaurants,
the weather and our fine
resources. Now they're talking
about our determination, our
stamina and our
people pulling together."*

ABOVE: Standing in the shadow of the
collapsed I-880 freeway, a stunned
President Bush utters a single word:
"Jesus." *Photo by Steve Ringman*

LEFT: Gawkers pour in to damaged areas to record the wreckage. *Photo by John O'Hara*

BELOW: San Francisco's Mayor Art Agnos gives out information to anxious residents at Marina Green. *Photo by Darcy Padilla*

ABOVE: Mayor Agnos praises weary Marina residents, saying "You have been magnificent in your response," but he draws boos when he cannot immediately provide a detailed list of buildings to be demolished. Inhabitants fear they will lose everything if they cannot get back inside before the demolitions. *Photo by Darcy Padilla*

LEFT: Marina residents await word on when they can go home. *Photo by Darcy Padilla*

What now?

The Bay Area took a deep breath and thought about tomorrow.

The next Monday would mean back to work for the first time in almost a week for tens of thousands of workers who had cheerfully obeyed instructions to stay away from downtown Oakland and San Francisco. More than 300,000 vehicles cross the Bay Bridge each day. Zero would cross on Monday.

But they would make out somehow.

RIGHT: The owner of a collapsed building questions Mayor Agnos. *Photo by Darcy Padilla*

LEFT: Some streets in the Marina resemble Europe during World War II. *Photo by Frederic Larson*

UPPER RIGHT: Watsonville residents share a tent on high school grounds. *Photo by Deanne Fitzmaurice*

LOWER RIGHT: Fearing aftershocks, a family stays outdoors, keeping warm by a barbecue fire and listening to a transistor radio. *Photo by Steve Castillo*

WATSONVILLE

Theresa Padilla
Newly homeless

"I'm sad and I'm scared."

Raoul Perez
Farm worker

"We have no place to live. The building cracked. It's hard, especially for the kids, because we have no gas, water, special things for kids."

TOP: Children staying in a park share soup donated by volunteers. *Photo by Deanne Fitzmaurice*

BOTTOM: Kids make instant friends when their families camp outdoors. *Photo by Chris Stewart*

RIGHT: A parade of shaken Watsonville residents march and pray for no more tremors. *Photo by Chris Stewart*

RIGHT:
Food from a refrigerator
spills onto a tilted floor
in the Santa Cruz
mountains. *Photo by
Deanne Fitzmaurice*

RIGHT:
The cleanup commences
in San Francisco.
*Photo by
John O'Hara*

SAN FRANCISCO

Jeffrey Kletsky
Marina District resident

"All of a sudden I have no control

over my life. The worst thing is not

knowing what will happen."

HOPE

OVERLEAF: A smile amid
the wreckage as
reconstruction begins.
Photo by Steve Castillo

Turning around

The people of Northern California were brave, many of them heroic. They were gallant in how they endured hardship and suffering; they gave one other a helping hand, bore up under their losses, smiled through their tears. They gave the rest of the world a plucky thumbs-up: We're OK, Jack. Takes more than 7.1 on the Richter scale to get us down.

Ten days after the quake, the San Francisco Giants and the Oakland Athletics resumed their interrupted World Series. A huge crowd at Candlestick Park paused to remember the dead and sang the corny old song "San Francisco," which celebrates the rebirth of the city after the quake of 1906. Twelve people honored for heroism threw out the ceremonial first pitches.

Then 62,000 fans went on to cheer baseball and the joy of being alive.

ABOVE AND RIGHT:
Ferries ply the bay, carrying commuters beneath the Bay Bridge, which is temporarily shut down. "This city has been through this before," said a resident. "We will rebuild."
Photos by Steve Ringman

Trey Bonetti
October 27, 1989

"Like life, baseball

has to go on."

ABOVE: A Giants fan dresses for the
occasion. "Once the game started, it
was as if the earthquake never
happened," said another delirious fan.
Photo by Mike Maloney

LEFT: At a resumed World Series, men
and women who were among the
heroes of the earthquake rescue effort
get ready to throw out the first ball.
Photo by Mike Maloney

LESSONS

By Randy Shilts

Days after the jolt, the first winter rains swept into the Bay Area and temperatures began to plunge.

October 17, 1989, had been a day of unseasonable warmth. The temperatures floated in the 80s; people wore tank tops and cutoffs, smug in the knowledge that only in California was nature so kind that in late October you could enjoy such heat.

Nature is the allure of California. Those who love money go to New York; those who lust for fame go to Los Angeles; those who love natural beauty come to San Francisco. But for the perfect harbor, the elegant coastline and the azure skies, we must pay. It's not exactly a Faustian bargain, but nature does exact a price.

It was to these and other thoughts that the collective consciousness of our region returned, again and again, when the rains and cold drove us back indoors, and we steeled ourselves for a disconsolate winter. The thoughts — and the fears — wouldn't fade as the hours after the temblor faded into days and then weeks.

We told our where-we-were-when-it-hit stories ad nauseam. Everybody knew somebody whose schedule had almost taken her to that ill-fated section of Interstate 880 during rush hour, and she had barely missed it. In less common stories, the kind we would retell for years to come, there was someone who had the misfortune to keep his appointment with destiny with macabre split-second precision. The question, usually unspoken, then lingered: Why her, why him? And, of course, why not me?

The external world busily tied up loose ends, making things neat again. Having thoroughly masticated the event for the national TV audience, the network anchors were the first to go. They boarded their white stretch limousines and drove away, awaiting the arrival of the next world event. In their final video reports, they usually summarized the earthquake with just four pictures: the lethal stretch of I-880 in Oakland, the deadliest roadway in American history; the apartment building in the Marina District, with its ornate Victorian crown, once four stories high, now just a few feet off the sidewalk; the broken Bay Bridge; and the pretty blond woman with the scarlet scarf in her hair, weeping, "We never really believed it would happen."

Every day, the subplots of the story inched further toward resolution. The last known bodies were pulled from the wreckage of the now-infamous Cypress structure of I-880; the damaged homes were razed in the Marina District; the homeless of Santa Cruz began to find their way to shelter before the worst of the winter set in. Even in the Bay Area, the headlines returned to prosaic matters: commute problems, measures of aftershocks, legislative maneuvering on aid packages.

The *Sturm und Drang* of death and destruction passed. For all but a few thousand of the most directly affected, the Loma Prieta earthquake was gradually reduced to the mundane, a level with which we were all more comfortable. On street corners, vendors braved brisk November breezes and hawked their T-shirts: "I Survived the Great Earthquake of 1989." Such are our times; today's tragedy is tomorrow's T-shirt.

Still, Loma Prieta posed troubling questions, not only for the Bay Area and not only about earthquakes, but also for the nation and for the great social conflicts that churn beneath the seemingly tranquil surface of society.

In this sense, the catastrophe on I-880 emerged as the social and even political metaphor of our era. For all the official shuffling and buck-passing that followed the disaster, a few facts about the freeway were horribly clear.

First, the collapse of I-880 surprised few of the engineers who had studied the freeway's seismic safety. The roadway had only done what they had warned it might do; it pancaked under the stress of the quake. Politicians and editorial writers howled for accountability, as if beheading the official who allowed traffic on the structure would settle everything.

That was too simple an answer. Bringing to justice the individual who approved use of the doomed span is like blaming a lynching on the man who tied the noose. Just as the whole mob is guilty in a lynching, guilty too for I-880 were all the parts of the body politic that created the environment in which a dangerous freeway was not repaired.

The bigger rub in the I-880 disaster is this: A net to catch all the possible villains in the freeway collapse must be cast across the country.

In 1980, 1984 and 1988, Americans elected federal administrations that were committed to one overriding priority: reducing taxes by limiting government and holding down social spending. As Ronald Reagan was fond of repeating, "Government isn't the solution, it's the problem." This philosophy led to severe budget cuts on all domestic spending programs. Such programs included agencies that perform all kinds of obscure little tasks, such as seismic safety for highways. Reports were quick to come from Washington that federal highway safety agencies to protect roads from things like earthquakes had had their budgets drastically slashed since President Reagan took office in 1981. Funding was reduced further under President Bush.

Bureaucrats in Washington argued that, ultimately, highway safety programs are the responsibility of state officials. That's true. However, the state administration has been as loath as the federal administration to spend money and launch any initiative that might cause a tax increase. The effects of this posturing are evident in much more than broken highways.

Since California voters gave birth to the "Tax Revolt" with the passage of Proposition 13 in 1978, the state's infrastructure has been eroding. Bridges and freeways, hospitals and schools, sewers and water projects are beginning to wear down for lack of repairs. A governor's task force put the cost of needed repairs to the public works of California alone at more than $50 billion.

Politicians are not courageously racing to propose construction programs and the new taxes to pay for them. That would be political suicide. After all, we live in an era when the only national vision a candidate needs to express to become Leader of the Free World can be articulated in just six words: "Read my lips: no new taxes."

Read the logical conclusion of such political theology in the girders twisted like spaghetti above the Oakland landscape and among the boulders of concrete that entombed 1½ miles of rush-hour traffic.

Tax rates in the United States are among the lowest of all the world's industrialized democracies, while incomes are among the highest. Yet Americans protect every cent of their paychecks, unwilling to part with an extra percentage point in taxes and rebuffing any politician who does not promise even smaller revenue collections for future years. The lust for a second VCR and a longer luxury sedan has overwhelmed concerns about tedious issues such as infrastructure. We expect to drive on freeways that don't collapse in earthquakes, but we don't expect to pay for the programs to keep them in repair.

In this sense, what happened to the physical infrastructure in the Bay Area in just 15 seconds is what will be happening to America's social infrastructure over the next 15 years.

Americans want an educational system that competes internationally, but they're not willing to pay teachers a decent salary. We spend $1,500 for home security systems, but we're unwilling to put the same money into job training programs that could give that midnight burglar a more honest calling. We tell pollsters we want health care available to every citizen, but we'll never elect a politician who would enact such a program, because that would mean raising taxes.

On a fundamental level, we're less afraid of the problem than of the solution and what it would cost. This national selfishness will haunt America for decades.

To say that this is the only lesson of the Loma Prieta quake, however, would be to tell only half the story. As if to underscore the bipolar nature of the contemporary American spirit, the other half of this saga is told in tales of gallantry.

The West Oakland residents who crawled into the crumbling freeway to rescue trapped drivers defined heroism. As Northern California pulled together in those first days after the earthquake, no self-sacrifice was too large if it would help a neighbor. The region's response to the tragedy personified altruism and compassion.

If such individual acts of benevolence could become the social norm and spread across the country, maybe America would experience the political revitalization to which so many in the Bay Area looked forward in the first weeks after the quake.

On one level, a lesson from the I-880 and bridge collapse was that better-funded seismic safety programs and highway repair would have prevented the tragedy. The other lesson is that Americans are capable of heroic deeds when so called upon. We still have the moral resources to commit ourselves to the political deeds that can reverse our national decline.

On an individual level, for those who lived through the tremors, the psychic aftershakes continue, offering valuable personal lessons.

For all our modern amenities, we are psychologically ill

prepared for events such as earthquakes. We live in a humanistic age in which we have down-sized the mysteries of the universe to a human scale. The vastness of the heavens, the depths of the oceans, the molecular structures of the cells that compose our bodies — all have been gauged to man's measure.

With so few mysteries to baffle us and so little out of our control, we are the masters of our universe. Feeling invulnerable in our cars of steel and glass, we speed between deals and destinations. Concerns of mortality are most commonly counted in cholesterol levels. The part of ourselves we are most apt to measure is our waistline.

And then it strikes. The earth moves. The timbers creak, slowly at first, and then louder, until it seems the floor is roaring at you. When will it stop? Will it stop? Oh my God, is this The Big One? Will I live?

The truth, so often denied, returns: Our well-ordered lives can be crushed in a few seconds.

Relieved to still be alive, we venture from our doorways to the street; for the first time, we meet the neighbor we always ignored.

For weeks after the earthquake, people would pause as they walked across the room and tremulously ask, "Did you feel that? Was that an aftershock?" Sometimes it was, but most commonly it was nothing, a phantom quiver that reflected the continuing uncertainty as to whether the ground was indeed firm and whether it would ever be so firm again.

Perhaps people in the Middle Ages, before our humanistic era, had an easier time dealing with such phenomena as earthquakes. Their universe had an omniscient God and an energetic Satan, and a ranked and orderly chain of being from archangels down to the lowliest crawling crea-

ture. In a world guided by forces beyond human measure, events defying mortal dimensions, such as earthquakes, seemed less foreign; helplessness was not so alien an emotion. Given our times, however, disasters are followed by teams of psychologists chatting about post-traumatic stress disorder.

"It makes you think," people said, again and again. They never had to say what it made you think about. The verb needed no object, because anyone who lived through the earthquake understood. It just made you think.

You began to measure yourself in new ways, such as in the depth of your relationships. Existence, you knew, depended not upon making it to the next appointment but upon having an acquaintance, or even a stranger, willing to dig you out of the rubble. Quality of life was determined not by the value of mutual funds but by how well neighbors took care of one another. Mortality became a pressing concern, forcing people to re-evaluate their lives. Was an unfulfilling job worth it, even for just a few more years, considering your life could end instantly on some random roadway?

Perspective also returned, perspective about what is real and what is ephemeral. For all the hubris born of our technological age, there was the realization that Nature has the upper hand. She always has and she always will; she reminds us rarely, particularly in this blessed part of the world, but when she does rise up, it can be with harrowing fury and horrible consequence. Long after the last debris has been cleaned and the Great Earthquake of 1989 has faded into history, that will be the lasting lesson, imprinted upon the memories of millions:

We are very small creatures, still.

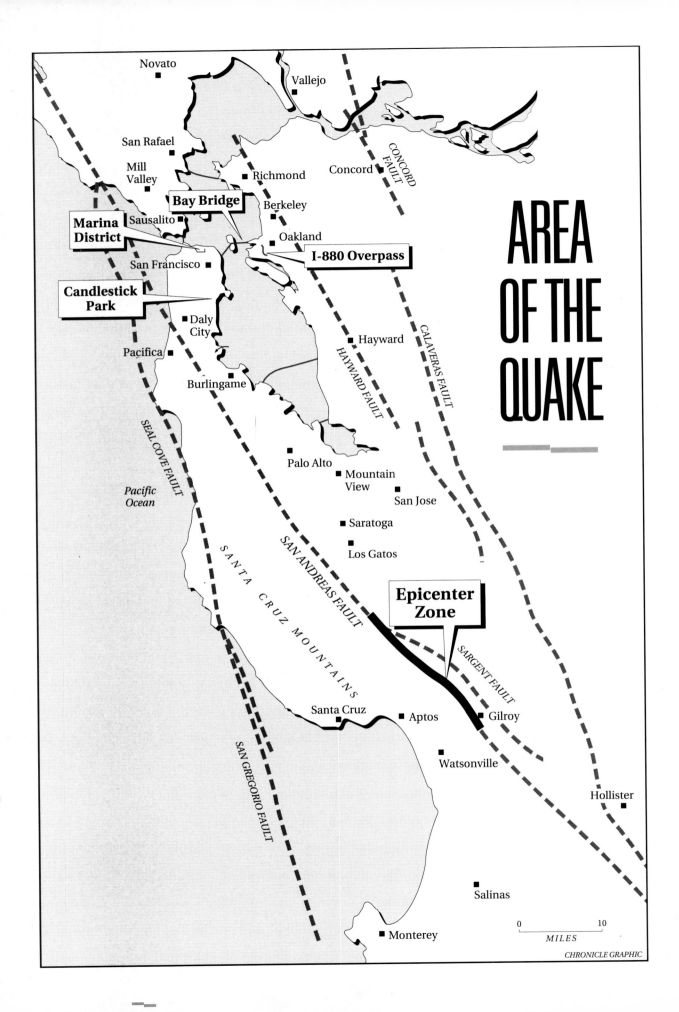

Novato

Vallejo

San Rafael

Mill Valley

Richmond

Concord

CONCORD FAULT

Bay Bridge

Berkeley

Sausalito

Marina District

Oakland

I-880 Overpass

San Francisco

Candlestick Park

Daly City

Hayward

HAYWARD FAULT

CALAVERAS FAULT

Pacifica

SEAL COVE FAULT

Burlingame

Palo Alto

Mountain View

San Jose

Pacific Ocean

Saratoga

Los Gatos

SANTA CRUZ MOUNTAINS

SAN ANDREAS FAULT

Epicenter Zone

SARGENT FAULT

Santa Cruz

Aptos

Gilroy

Watsonville

SAN GREGORIO FAULT

Hollister

Salinas

0   10
MILES

Monterey

CHRONICLE GRAPHIC

AREA OF THE QUAKE

Much of The Chronicle's editorial staff was involved in covering the earthquake and its aftermath, including:

Sue Adolphson
Calvin Ahlgren
John Aiello
Bill Arnold
Nanette Asimov

Kenneth Baker
Mark Barabak
Jim Barrios
Dale Basye
Bernie Beck
Richard Beckerley
Jamie Beckett
Andrea Behr
Tom Benet
Mike Bigelow
Tony Bizjak
Craig Black
Kathy Bodovitz
John Boring
Jack Breibart
Jim Brewer
Robert Britton
Charles Burress
David Bush

Herb Caen
Tracy Caldwell
Mark Camps
William Carlsen
John Carman
Mike Carmean
Jody Carpenter
Jo Carrasco
Jerry Carroll
Jon Carroll
Steve Castillo
Ken Castle
Ron Chan
Harriet Chiang
Marianne Chin
Lisa Chung
Don Clark
Myra Cole
Bruce Colvin
Robert Commanday
William Cone
Dean Congbalay
Ken Conner
Bill Cooney
Anthony Cooper
Karola Craib
Will Crain
Jonathan Curiel
John Curley
Diane Curtis
Jacob Curtis

Rob Davila
Rick Del Vecchio
Harre Demoro
Georgeanne Dennison
Charlie Denson
Phelps Dewey

David Dietz
Elliot Diringer
Louis Dolinsky
Thomas Dotson
Jim Doyle
Terry Dunlap

John Eckhouse
Dave Einstein
Edward Epstein
Laura Evenson

Christine Feldhorn
David Finkelstein
Tom FitzGerald
Deanne Fitzmaurice
Bob Fleming
Gary Fong
Hal Foster
Margo Freistadt
Iris Frost

Aida Gamez
Leah Garchik
Dawn Garcia
Richard Geiger
Dan Geisin
William German
Rita Gibbs
Tom Gilmore
Bob Graham
Tom Graham
Helen Green
Leonard Greene
Leslie Guevarra
Robert Gunnison
Leslie Guttman

Rob Haeseler
Liz Hafalia
Wes Haley
Carl Hall
Martin Halstuk
Jesse Hamlin
Mike Harris
Julia Hawkins
Richard Hemp
Leba Hertz
Jim Hicks
Andrea Himes
David Hipschman
Mark Hokoda
Patricia Holt
Art Hoppe
Sally Hosley
Ken Howe
David Hyams

Dorine Iacono
Erik Ingram

Bruce Jenkins
Clarence Johnson
Jennifer Johnson
Lonn Johnston
Rodney Jones
Eric Jungerman

Dorothy Kantor
Tom Keane
Mike Keiser
Marybeth Kerrigan

Vlae Kershner
Marshall Kilduff
Tom Kimball
Pam King
Betty Kirkendall
Marshall Kirkland
David Kleinberg
Rob Knies
Joshua Kosman
Bruce Krefting

Perry Lang
Fred Larson
Mick LaSalle
Don Lattin
Kevin Leary
Bonnie Lemons
Ed Lempinen
Dianne Levy
Tom Levy
Karen Liberatore
Larry Liebert
Kimball Livingston
Betsy Lombard
Arthur Louis
Greg Lucas
Patricia Luchak
Liz Lufkin
Mark Lundgren

Michael McCabe
Sharon McCormick
Paul McHugh
Doug Mackey
Ramon McLeod
Regan McMahon
Lynda MacNamara
Kathy McNulty
Ena Macrae
Vince Maggiora
August Maggy
Mike Maloney
Mary Ann Mariner
Bruce Martin
Steve Massey
Alyx Meltzer
Laura Merlo
Ira Miller
Judy Miller
Torri Minton
David Moore
Tom Murray

Tim Neagle
Hulda Nelson
C.W. Nevius
Tony Newhall
Shann Nix
Barr Nobles
Carl Nolte
Carol Norek

John O'Hara
Lori Olszewski
Steve Outing

Darcy Padilla
Mike Palmer
Tina Pania
Jim Parkinson
Bill Pates

Jeff Pelline
Jackie Pels
Kathleen Pender
Gail Persily
Richard Pestorich
Charles Petit
Joel Pimsleur
Leslie Pittel
Robert Popp

Ray Ratto
Pam Reasner
Kate Regan
Jeff Reinking
Kathleen Rhodes
Steve Ringman
Jerry Roberts
Michael Robertson
Jack Robinson
Jim Rose
Art Rosenbaum
Daniel Rosenheim
Chuck Ross
Steve Rubenstein
Sabin Russell

Marc Sandalow
John Schneidawind
Tim Schreiner
Stephen Schwartz
Joe Shea
Peter Shifter
Randy Shilts
Sharon Silberstein
Peter Sinton
Amy Smith
Bill Smith
Derelle Smith
Philip Smith
Scott Sommerdorf
Peter Stack
Pat Steger
Ruthe Stein
Chris Stewart
Pearl Stewart
Otis Stillwell
Judy Stone
Kris Strawser
Brian Sulkis
Pat Sullivan
Peter Sussman

Gary Swan
Susan Sward

Jane Taber
Michael Taylor
Jerry Telfer
Allan Temko
Ray Tessler
Richard T. Thieriot
Pamela Thoms
Ron Thomas
Bob Thompson
Marilyn Tucker
David Tuller

Marsha Vande Berg
Bill Van Niekerken
Carole Vernier
Jack Viets
Deborah Villa
Frank Viviano

Bill Wallace
Brant Ward
Eric Ward
Rufus Watkins
Lloyd Watson
Mary Jo Webb
Bernie Weiner
Evelyn White
Sam Whiting
John Wildermuth
George Williamson
Matthew Wilson
Steven Winn
Nancy Wong
Bill Workman
Rosalie Muller Wright
Gail Wrixon

Michael Yamamoto
Lyle York

Marian Zailian
Maitland Zane
Tanja Zimmerman

This book was edited by Lyle York and Christine Feldhorn of The Chronicle staff and Jay Schaefer of Chronicle Books.

ABOVE: Deprived of electricity for two days, the staff of The Chronicle put out two special earthquake editions by flashlight. *Photo by Steve Ringman*